MW01697904

MINUTE MEDITATIONS

Meeting God in Everyday Experiences

Michele T. Huey

Ampelos Press
Drexel Hill, PA

Minute Meditations
Meeting God in Everyday Experiences
Copyright © 2000 Michele T. Huey

ISBN 0-9661305-4-5

Cover design by J.L. Hardesty, Images Unlimited
Cover photo and inside illustration Digital imagery ® copyright 1999 PhotoDisc, Inc.

Published by
Ampelos Press
316 Blanchard Road
Drexel Hill, Pennsylvania 19026

All rights reserved. No part of this book may be reproduced in whole or in part without written permission from the author (121 Homestead Lane, Glen Campbell, PA 15742 or email mthuey@penn.com), except by a reviewer who may quote brief passages in a review; nor may any part of this book be reproduced, stored in a retrieval system, or transmitted in any form or by any means electronic, mechanical, including photocopying, recording, or other, without permission in writing from the author, except as provided by USA copyright law.

Scripture quotations noted KJV are from the King James Version.

Scripture quotations marked (NIV) are from The Holy Bible: NEW INTERNATIONAL VERSION. Copyright © 1978 by the New York International Bible Society. Used by permission of Zondervan Bible Publishers.

Scripture quotations marked (NKJV) are taken from the New King James Version. Copyright © 1979, 1980, 1982 by Thomas Nelson, Inc. Used by permission. All rights reserved.

Scripture quotations marked (NLT) are taken from the *Holy Bible*, New Living Translation, copyright © 1996. Used by permission of Tyndale House Publishers, Inc., Wheaton, Illinois 60189, U.S.A. All rights reserved.

Scripture quotations marked (TLB) are taken from *The Living Bible* copyright © 1971. Used by permission of Tyndale House Publishers, Inc., Wheaton, Illinois 60189. All rights reserved.

Printed in the United States of America

To Elizabeth Jelich,
My dearest Aunt Betty,
Who has always believed in me,
Always been there for me,
And always, always,
Loved me just as I was,
From the moment I took my first breath,
To when I grew into an inquisitive, noisy child,
Who turned into an awkward teen
Searching for my place in the world,
To when I became a young mother
Struggling to keep an identity,
To when I became a grandmother,
A "baba" myself.

Places

The place where
I most long to be
is at my Brother's feet,
listening,
learning,
loving.

But most often,
I find myself
huddled in my Father's lap,
my head resting softly
on His shoulder,
His Father's arms around me.

I feel the gentle caress
of the Hand that leads me
when I am strong enough
to be off and running
once again.

As the deer pants for streams of water,
so I long for you, O God.
Psalm 42:1 NLT

Foreword

Have you ever met someone you immediately felt comfortable with, someone so real and down-to-earth that you knew you could be yourself, too?

Michele has the gift of creating an immediate bond with her readers. Her openness, honesty, and transparency will make you laugh and cry.

But this book is not about Michele, as much as it is about the God she seeks to know and serve. His promise to Michele, and to you and to me, is that He knows the plans He has for us. And they are good plans, to give us a future and a hope (see Jeremiah 29:11). "You will find me when you seek me," He promises, "if you look for me in earnest" (Jeremiah 29:13 TLB).

It's amazing but true! The God who created everything that exists desires for us to know Him personally. May you meet Him through these "minute meditations" and discover, in new and life-changing ways, His presence in your everyday experiences.

Marlene Bagnull

First Things First

"I am the LORD your God. . . . You shall have no other gods before me."

—Exodus 20:2-3 NIV

"Take time to smell the lilacs," begins a poem I have framed in my bedroom. I put it where I hoped I would see it every day. Perhaps it would remind me to slow down, I thought. But here I am, again, with too many irons in the fire.

Last week I walked out of two stores without all my purchases. As usual, I was in a hurry, my mind on a million and one things.

I rush to get out the door each day, only to grumble when I get stuck behind someone who slows me down. I count the number of grocery items the person in front of me in the express line has in his cart. I find myself checking my watch when I meet up with someone I haven't seen in a while and we start chatting. Even during my quiet time, my thoughts wander off to the things I have to do that day instead of focusing on God.

Sometimes I feel as though my life is like the whirlwind, earthquake, and fire Elijah experienced on the mountain. And I don't like it one bit! Like Elijah, I need to rediscover that God is not in the tumultuous, hectic pace I often set for myself. He's in the stillness I find in the predawn darkness, before the world and all its demands begin to stir.

There are many ways God can get nudged out of first place in our lives, and busyness is one of them—even busyness for Him. I need to remind myself that putting God first means taking the time to get to know Him by spending time with Him and allowing Him to order my day. He will give me the nudge I need to take time to smell the lilacs, hear the whisper of the wind in the trees, watch the cloud shadows skip across a windswept field, enjoy a blazing sunset in the middle of getting supper, or savor a cup of tea in my robe by the fireplace on a cold winter morn. Those are the things that put me in touch with their Creator and calm my raging spirit within.

That's when I hear Him best—when my heart and mind are finally still. Then I can move forward into a day that I've already given over to the One who truly has first place in my life.

Slow me down, Lord. Amen.

ANOTHER MINUTE

Read & meditate on 1 Kings 19:9-13.

The Right Choice

"Who do you say I am?"
—Mark 8:29 NIV

I've always had a hard time making up my mind. If I went shopping for a dress and saw two that I liked, I usually bought both of them. Many times I'd come home from shopping trips with two pairs of shoes, two tops, and two skirts or two pair of jeans—all because I couldn't make a choice. I'd even try the "Eenie, meenie, minie, moe" routine, but when I'd come to the end of the rhyme, I couldn't decide whether to say, "you are *it*" or "you are *out*." Even now, I cringe at the thought of deciding between two seemingly equal options.

There was a time, however, when making the right choice wasn't all that difficult. That was back when I thought religion was something I had to do. Even then I always strove to reach beyond the ritual I thought I had to perform to the God whom I sensed loved me and cared for me a personal way. When I finally had to choose between *religion*—all those things I thought I had to do to get right with God—and *faith*—believing that what God's Son did on Calvary's cross was all I needed to get right with Him—the choice wasn't hard. I never hesitated for a fraction of a second. And I've never looked back and tried to second-guess the most important decision I've ever made.

When Jesus Christ, God's Son, walked this earth, He called people to make their own choices. "Who do you say that I am?" He once asked His disciples. It was the unspoken question in His encounters with Nicodemus, the woman at the well, Pontius Pilate, and the thief on the cross. All had to answer. Where they would spend eternity depended on the choice they made.

How about you? Have you made the right choice yet?

Thank You, Father, that all I ever needed to do to earn heaven was done on the cross by Your Son, Jesus. Amen.

ANOTHER MINUTE

Read & meditate on Luke 23:32-43.

Real Love

Love . . . is not self-seeking.
—1 Corinthians 13:4-5 NIV

The reporter on television was conducting on-the-street interviews, asking people what they thought was the number one Valentine's Day present: flowers, candy, or jewelry? Considering I can't remember even getting a card from my husband on Valentine's Day in all our twenty-five years of marriage, I ignored the broadcast and concentrated on preparing the Bible lesson I was to teach the next day.

"What do *you* think is the number one gift?" my husband asked me.

I looked at him for a good ten seconds before I deadpanned, "Nothing."

A look of hurt flickered across his face before he smiled and said, "Okay, so you want nothing for Valentine's Day?"

You dummy, I silently scolded myself, as I shrugged and went back to my lesson planning. *Now look what you've done.* The next time I looked up from my books, he was sound asleep in his chair.

What do I think is the number one gift? I asked myself, remembering the wildflowers he often brings home during the summer. Those tiger lilies mean more to me than any greenhouse rose. I thought of his patience and understanding when I have to work late.

Too often I've approached our marriage with an attitude of "What's in it for me?" rather than "What can I do for you?"

Real love "is not self-seeking" (1 Corinthians 13:5 NIV). "Love is patient, love is kind. It does not envy, it does not boast, it is not proud. It is not rude, . . . it is not easily angered, it keeps no record of wrongs. . . . It always trusts, always hopes, always perseveres" (1 Corinthians 13:4-7 NIV).

That's a pretty good description of my husband, I thought. What is the number one gift for Valentine's Day I'd like to receive? I already have it!

Thank You, Lord, for my husband. Amen.

ANOTHER MINUTE

Read & meditate on 1 Corinthians 13.

Of Moms and Homes

The eternal God is your refuge,
and underneath are the everlasting arms.
—Deuteronomy 33:27 NIV

One of the things I remember most about my mother was her love for the steel mill town where she grew up, married, and raised a family. Even when my dad lost his job in the mill due to massive layoffs and found another job half the state away, she refused to leave "good ol' Donora." Here she could find comfort and love in the lonely times when Dad was away. She could always scoot across the street to her mother's for a brief respite from raising three squabbling kids alone. And a little corner grocery store two doors up the street would extend her credit when the money was low and deliver when the list was long.

By the time her Alzheimer's disease was apparent, Dad had died, her mother was in a nursing home, and her children were raising families of their own. When she could no longer live alone, it fell upon me to move her furniture from the home she loved so dearly. I grieved not only for my own loss, but also for hers. She was leaving Donora for good.

One day, months later, I found a small, blue card with a Bible verse printed on it: "The eternal God is your dwelling place . . ." In my grief, I had forgotten the most important thing Mom ever taught me: What matters most is not our earthly home, but the one we have with God.

Dear God, thank You for the mother You gave me for the years I had her. Thank You for the assurance that she has a home in heaven with You forever. Amen.

ANOTHER MINUTE
Read & meditate on 2 Corinthians 4:16—5:1.

Mama's Hankie

I wasn't always tattered;
I wasn't always torn.
I didn't always look so limp,
So tired and forlorn.
Once my threads were crisper,
My colors seemed to glow;
But I was harsh against a face
When tears would start to flow.

So I traded in my beauty
For softer threads of years,
So I could fit into your hand
And gather all your tears.
So treasure all my careworn threads—
In time they'll fall apart;
And take with you the tenderness
And love that's in my heart.

Birthday Blues

For I am convinced that neither death nor life, neither angels nor demons, neither the present nor the future, nor any powers, neither height nor depth, nor anything else in all creation, will be able to separate us from the love of God that is in Christ Jesus our Lord.

—Romans 8:38-39 NIV

I plopped down on the sofa, exhausted after a long day of housework and caring for toddlers. It was my birthday, but there would be no cake, no ice cream, no family get-together. I was the one who usually planned such events, and I wasn't going to do all that extra work for myself.

"Some birthday," I muttered.

Birthdays were a lot more fun when I was growing up and there was someone around to make a big deal out of them and make me feel special. Not so anymore.

Dad was dead—buried on my twentieth birthday. Mom had Alzheimer's disease and didn't even know I existed. My brother and sister were busy raising their own families in other states. My husband worked thirteen-hour days and had neither the time nor the money even to buy me a card since I didn't give him much of an allowance after the bills were paid. And my kids were too little to do anything about my birthday blues.

Who wants to bake her own birthday cake? Certainly not me! The only party I'd have this year would be a pity party.

"Lord," I whispered into the now-quiet living room, "I feel so alone. Oh, I know it's silly, but today I just need to hear something special from You."

I opened my Bible to the day's meditation. As I read Romans 8:35-39, I heard the voice of the Creator of the universe whispering, *Michele, I love you.*

What a cure for the "Birthday Blues!"

Dear God, I love You, too.

ANOTHER MINUTE
Read & meditate on Romans 8:35-39.

Bad Hair Days

Everyone did what was right in his own eyes.
—Judges 21:25 NKJV

My hair is going through an adolescent stage," I announced to my hairdresser. "It won't do what I want it to do!"

Ever since I caught a cold and have been taking medication, my locks won't lay right. At first I blamed it on my hair being out of shape. So I carved some time out of my schedule and got it trimmed. It turned out a bit shorter than what I'm used to, but I like the feel of it. The only problem is that it still wants to do its own thing. I bought some spritz, but that only stiffened it more in its rebellion.

I figure I have two choices: Let it grow out, or cut more off. The first option will take time. Patience is not, however, one of my finer points. The second option I'm still considering, but I think I'll give it a week or so to see if it'll settle down any. In the meantime, life goes on—with or without bad hair days.

My stubborn hair reminds me of my own stubborn heart. I, too, go through stages of obedience and rebellion. During times of obedience, I set time aside daily to read the Bible and pray. God and I are on great terms. But then something happens—I get sick or busy or stressed when a situation doesn't turn out the way I want it to—and I find excuses to put off reading and praying.

"I just don't feel like it," I reason. "God understands." But the real reason I put God off during those times is that I'm pouting. I want my own way.

God, in His infinite patience, however, keeps working with those stubborn wisps in my nature until they finally come under His control. Sometimes He has to lop off those areas that give Him (and me) the most grief. But, little by little, He is shaping and trimming my inner nature so that someday I won't ever have to worry about bad hair days again.

Thank You, Lord, that You don't give up on me as easily as I give up on myself when life gets a little "hairy." Amen.

ANOTHER MINUTE
Read & meditate on Romans 8:1-17.

Minute Medication

"If I only touch his cloak, I will be healed."
—Matthew 9:21 NIV

I once read of a woman who donned a teddy bear costume and visited nursing homes giving hugs to the residents. The article reported that many of the lonely and withdraw residents "just melted" in the bear's arms and smiled for the first time in months.

A recent study suggested that couples who enjoy a loving relationship can better withstand the pressures of modern living and seem to have a higher resistance to illness. Another study, done in an orphanage, showed that babies who are touched affectionately fare better than ones who are never touched.

Touch—hugs, pats, caresses—are important to our physical, emotional, and mental well being. You can't love someone without touching them. My back rubs and goodnight hugs tell my children I love them. My reaching for my husband's hand tells him I love him.

When I come home after a hectic, stressful day, the first thing I want is a hug. When I want to encourage a friend, I pat him on the back. Touch says, "I love you." "I care about you."

When people came to Jesus for healing, He touched them and they were healed.

Touch still has the power to heal. Yet today, sadly enough, we distance ourselves from each other for fear of being misunderstood—or sued.

Now, I'm not going to go around touching everyone I meet. But I can encourage a friend, reassure a child, or show family members I love them without a single word. A loving touch is a "minute medication."

Dear Lord, show me someone who needs a hug today. Amen.

ANOTHER MINUTE
Read & meditate on Luke 8:43-48.

God and Me and a Bowl of Chicken Soup

"Ask, and it will be given to you."
—Matthew 7:7 NKJV

"Lord, when I get home, I could go for some good, old-fashioned, homemade chicken soup!"

I'd just delivered my second child by Caesarean section and was feeling weak, tired, and depressed. How I envied those women who had their babies naturally! They were up and about within a day. Not me. I'd be bedridden for a week in the hospital, then another week after I got home. For some reason, I just didn't bounce back after childbirth like others did.

I longed for my mother's homemade chicken soup which had always made me feel better. But Mom, a victim of Alzheimer's disease, lived with my sister two hundred miles away.

How am I going to take care of a newborn baby and an active toddler when I get home? I wondered. My husband couldn't take any more time off work. When my first child was born, Mom had spent a month with us, cleaning, washing, cooking, and making me chicken soup.

"I'll just have to do my best," I sighed, closing my eyes and settling deeper beneath the blanket.

A week later I was home in bed when my friend, Sharon, walked in carrying a tray.

"I brought you some homemade chicken soup," she announced.

"How did you know I wanted homemade chicken soup?" I asked her. "I never told anyone."

She grinned. Putting the tray on the nightstand, she said, "By the way, the ladies in our Bible study group signed up to bring one meal a day to your family while you're still in bed this week. We figured supper would be the best time for you. Is that all right?"

I nodded, feeling awed that the God who runs the universe would actually answer a prayer for chicken soup.

That was twenty years ago. Many times since then I've wondered if God heard my prayers. But then I remember when I felt His love in my friend's bowl of homemade chicken soup.

Dear God, open my eyes to the many ways You tell me You love me. Amen.

ANOTHER MINUTE

Read & meditate on Matthew 6:25-34.

House or Home?

Unless the LORD builds the house,
its builders labor in vain.
—Psalm 127:1 NIV

Twenty years ago when we began digging the foundation for our house, our plan was to build as we had the cash to pay for the next step. But never did we consider that two decades later, we'd still be living in an unfinished house.

It didn't bother me when the kids were little. No matter that David, our youngest, glued his drawings to the wall as we were rushing to get to Bible school on time one summer morning, or that he decorated the bathroom door with animal stickers. And when thirty kids trooped into my living room each week for Good News Club, I didn't go ballistic if Kool-Aid spilled on the carpet. Our time, energy, and money went into raising our three children. Bringing them up right was more important than siding the house, putting a roof over the patio, laying new carpeting, or buying new doors for the bedrooms and closets.

But now two of the three have grown up and moved out, and my husband seems more interested in heading out to the woods with his bird dog or to the ball field with David. And David doesn't seem as embarrassed as I am when he brings his friends to "Huey's half-finished house," as I call it.

Somewhere along the line, my perspective shifted—I see

the house and have lost sight of the home. Discontentment crowds out the joy I once felt.

I need to remind myself that the foundation of the Huey home is not blocks and mortar; it is Jesus Christ. That we are not surrounded merely by walls made of drywall, insulation, Celotex, and black paper; God Himself is a shield around us (see Psalm 3:3). And over us is not just a roof, but His love.

Yes, I still dream of finishing my house someday. But what is a house but four walls and a roof? It's the faith, hope, and love inside that are far more important. For they are what make up a home.

Father, when I begin to get discouraged about my unfinished house, remind me that the house is only temporary. But the home we establish in Your name will be passed through the generations. Amen.

ANOTHER MINUTE

Read & meditate on Psalm 127.

Stuck Again

Be still before the LORD and wait patiently for him.
—Psalm 37:7 NIV

Living in the country has its challenges, especially in the winter when the driveway is all but blown shut. I've never really had much trouble getting in the lane and up the driveway to my house, even with a two-wheel drive vehicle. A good running start is all I need to get through all but the deepest drifts. The only time I have any trouble is when I'm forced to slow down.

That's what happened one evening after it had snowed most of the day. Coming up the slight hill of my driveway, I had to slow down because one of our dogs decided to accompany me—trotting, right in front of the car, at his own leisurely pace. I tooted the horn, but the mutt went no faster.

Sure enough, about ten feet shy of my parking space, I spun out and could go no farther. But instead of leaving the car where it was, I tried to get it up closer to the house where it belonged. I didn't want to walk any farther than I had to. So I backed up, and backed up, and backed up—until I backed up right off the road!

The car was stuck in knee-deep snow. I could not go forward or backward. And now I had to walk two hundred feet to the house and warmth.

I really should have known better. I'd done the same thing with the van a few years back. Same ditch, too. You'd think I'd learn. All I had to do was wait and let my husband park the car after he cleared the driveway. But I didn't want to wait. I wanted my car in my parking space *now*.

Sometimes I run ahead of God, too. Rather than trust Him to work things out in His own time, I take matters in my own hands and kind of help Him along. But instead of making things better, my efforts just complicate the situation more. Then I have to confess my impatience and lack of trust, and ask my heavenly Father to undo the damage I've done. It's only when I let go and let Him work that I become "unstuck."

Help me, Father, to sense Your guidance as I plow through life. Amen.

ANOTHER MINUTE
Read & meditate on Genesis 16.

But those who wait on the LORD
Shall renew their strength . . .
They shall run and not be weary,
They shall walk and not faint.
Isaiah 40:31 NKJV

A Heart of Wisdom

So teach us to number our days,
that we may gain a heart of wisdom.
—Psalm 90:12 NKJV

Two days before Tax Day I was sorting through nearly a year's worth of clutter in my study, hunting for this year's tax forms.

Ever since I started working full time as a feature writer for my local newspaper, my filing method has been "drop it and run." The mounds of newspapers (I save everything I write), snapshots, receipts, insurance papers, canceled checks, bank statements, manuscripts, projects I've started but haven't finished, and whatever else I don't want to pitch mingle with dust and cobwebs—an avalanche waiting to happen if I rush past too fast. Avoiding the mess was impossible; the study is an open area right at the top of the steps. The view greeted me the first thing every morning and the last thing every night.

What bothered me most was that the disorganization was a reflection on me. That room was an unpleasant reminder of how far I'd slipped beneath my own standards—all because I took on more than I could realistically accomplish.

Living life in the fast lane has its price. We're in too much of a hurry to get as much done as we can to take the time to enjoy what we are doing, to savor the sunset, to linger over a cup of tea. Kind of like the "puddle ducks" and "divers."

A puddle duck snatches as much as he can on or just beneath the surface of the water. A diver, however, delves into the depths because that's where the best nourishment can be found.

I've been too much like the puddle duck, living life on the surface—rushing through meals, prayer time, Bible reading, family time, fun time, and snatching only superficial enjoyment. I need to ask God each day to give me the wisdom to balance my time and commitments so that I can get back to being a "diver" once again.

Dear God, grant me the wisdom to know when to say yes and when to say no. May I do each day what You want me to do. Nothing less. Nothing more. Amen.

ANOTHER MINUTE

Read and meditate on Psalm 90.

Donut Undoings

And God is faithful; he will not let you be tempted beyond what you can bear. But when you are tempted, he will also provide a way out so that you can stand up under it.

—1 Corinthians 10:13 NIV

My latest downfall began with a donut. When my forever hungry twelve-year-old son asked if we could stop for donuts after church on Sunday, I planned on getting only six. I figured he and his father could easily down three each. None for me since I can't eat anything with sugar. It makes me sick.

Usually I send the kids in with the money, but this time, since he was the only one with us, I accompanied him myself. Big mistake! The salesgirl pointed out that "for only a dollar more, you can get a whole dozen." I never could pass up a bargain, so, like a kid poring over a Christmas catalog, I studied the racks of sweets.

"One coconut-covered chocolate donut can't hurt," I reasoned. "It can't have *that* much sugar in it."

So one coconut-covered chocolate donut went into the box. Then the skinny, old-fashioned glazed because I figured it, too, had a lower sugar content than the fatter ones. On the way home, I chowed down the chocolate donut and shared the old-fashioned glazed with my husband out of guilt.

No thunder rolled, no lightening zapped because I caved in. But it was easier to raid the cookie jar on Monday, Tuesday, and Wednesday, even though I was beginning to feel the effects of the sugar—tiredness, irritability, achiness, and a craving for more sweets.

Sugar's effects on my body are no different than sin's effects on my soul. Nursing a grudge, listening to gossip, or stretching the truth may all seem harmless at first, but can poison my spirit and interfere with my relationship with God. Saying no in the first place makes it a lot easier to stay healthy—physically *and* spiritually.

Dear God, remind me that, big or small, a donut is still a donut. Help me to refuse that first bite. Amen.

ANOTHER MINUTE
Read & meditate on James 1:12-17.

Someday You'll Understand

"Honor your father and your mother."
—Exodus 20:12 NIV

I came across Dad's letter while rummaging though the bookcase for some now-forgotten item. The slightly yellowed envelope bore a State College postmark. I smiled softly. I didn't even know I'd saved it.

Settling on the game room carpet as snowflakes whirled in the winter wind outside, I reverently unfolded the letter, typewritten on motel stationery.

My dear Michele, it began. *Perhaps by now you are over the mad spell at me for scolding you last night. . . .*

My mind drifted back to a mid-summer night when I was fifteen. The warm summer sky sparkled with a thousand pin-lights as my friends and I walked through town. It was just the kind of night that holds magic for a teenage girl on the brink of growing up. Heady with all the freedom and fun, I'd neglected to call my parents to tell them I'd be late. By the time I climbed the porch steps, it was past midnight. Dad waited at the door.

This is the first time you ever stayed out late without calling and letting us know your whereabouts, the letter continued. *I was actually sick with worry after walking up to the bazaar and not finding you there. By that time I was imagining everything.*

I couldn't remember Dad ever being so angry with me before. After an ugly scene, I stormed up to my bedroom, grounded for two weeks. The next day Dad seemed to have gotten over his anger, but I treated him with icy silence. By the time he left for work Monday morning, I still hadn't spoken to him. Since Dad worked out of town through the week, I knew I wouldn't see him until Friday. The letter came Wednesday.

As I read Dad's words that long-ago day, my stubborn resistance melted away as a father's love triumphed over teen-age pride. One moment of panic, I realized, doesn't cancel out years of steadfast love. Four years later, Dad died.

It is so hard for a parent to be cross with a child, but sometimes it is necessary for your own good, he wrote. *Perhaps when you have children of your own, you will understand how we feel.*

I thought of my own three children. They'd all had me frantic with worry and fear at times as I imagined the worst. "Yes, Dad," I whispered softly, holding his letter close to my heart. "I understand."

Thank You, Father, for parents who loved me enough to discipline me when I needed it. Help me to be a parent worthy of being respected, valued, and honored. Amen.

ANOTHER MINUTE

Read & meditate on Hebrews 12:5-11.

A Man of Integrity

The integrity of the upright will guide them.
—Proverbs 11:3 NKJV

My father inspected state buildings that were under construction, making sure the contractors followed the blueprints. Having worked construction himself when he was younger, he knew too well how corners could be cut and a building's integrity undermined. He refused many a contractor's overtures, often gifts of liquor stashed in the back seat of his car. His colleagues soon recognized he could not be bought. He would not allow his personal integrity to be undermined.

"Integrity" comes from two Latin words that together mean "untouched, whole, entire." These two Latin roots also give us "integrate," which means "to weave or blend separate entities into a working whole or unit."

Personal integrity cannot be put on and off like a garment. Rather it is woven into the moral fabric of our lives over time. We weave it in each time we keep a promise or tell the truth no matter what it costs us, whether it's claiming all our income on our tax return, returning extra change we have received by mistake, or paying the difference when we are undercharged. We weave it in each time we admit our mistakes and take responsibility for our words and actions.

The U.S. Marines say they are looking for a few good men,

but all it takes is one man like my father to influence the world around him.

Lord, let me be that man!

ANOTHER MINUTE

Read & meditate on Nehemiah 5:14-19.

Better is the poor who walks in his integrity
than one who is perverse in his ways
though he be rich.
Proverbs 28:6 NKJV

Contentment Crisis

Be content with such things as you have. For He Himself has said, "I will never leave you nor forsake you."

—Hebrews 13:5 NKJV

"Lord, how can I be contented with what I have when what I have is either broken, worn out, or running on a prayer?"

I was in another one of my grumbling moods. Everywhere I looked, it seemed, something needed fixed or replaced. My range had one good burner, and the oven's temperature shot up a hundred degrees within seconds. The downstairs toilet ran constantly unless shut off by hand, and the hot water heater practically boiled the water at times. Other times we shivered in cold showers. Stuffing oozed out of every pillow in the house, and the dog had clawed up my bedspread.

Is this another one of God's lessons in patience? I wondered.

Then, while I was reading, a phrase seemed to jump off the page and address all my complaints: "Being is more important than having." Because I was putting having before being, I was discontented, joyless, and grumpy. What I needed was an attitude shift.

I could still cook on one burner, bake casseroles, and broil chicken. Even if the showers were occasionally cold, I had a warm bed to sleep in, no mortgage, and people who love me. What's more, I have a heavenly Father who promises to provide for all of my needs (see Philippians 4:19).

I still have problems being content when something else goes to the dogs. But as I view the tiger lilies my husband and children picked for me and feel a warm tenderness tug at my heart, I know I'm finally beginning to learn.

When something breaks down, dear Lord, remind me of what still works. Amen.

ANOTHER MINUTE

Read & meditate on Philippians 4:10-13.

Runaway Truck

If you keep your mouth shut,
you will stay out of trouble.
—Proverbs 21:23 NLT

"Who's coming up the driveway?" my youngest son wondered one morning when he came down for breakfast. I glanced out the dining room window. Sure enough, headlights pierced the morning mist halfway up the lane. Who could it be? At 6:30 a.m., we weren't expecting anyone.

"That's my company truck!" my oldest son, Todd, shrieked as he shot out the door in his stocking feet. He'd started the engine earlier to give it time to warm up while he got ready for work.

I'd noticed a week before that he'd parked it in the yard with a sledge hammer under the rear tire. "That's my parking brake," he explained when I'd asked him about the handle sticking out from under the tire.

Apparently, his "emergency brake" wasn't working now! The driverless truck slowly rolled backwards down the small hill of our lane. A few hair-raising minutes later, Todd parked the runaway truck sideways across the driveway and returned to the house.

"Don't you have an emergency brake?" I asked.

"Mom," he said in his best I'm-trying-to-be-patient-with-you tone, "that's a standard."

As if that explained everything. Not wanting to argue, I said nothing more. I've learned that keeping my mouth shut at times is better than spouting off motherly words of wisdom or pointing out the error of my offspring's thinking. Sometimes my kids really do know more than me about things. Other times they just aren't ready to hear what I have to say. So I say nothing.

But I'm not always so wise. Sometimes I let anger and frustration build up until, like that runaway truck, I'm rolling faster and faster towards disaster. I need to put on the "emergency brake" and breathe a quick prayer before I say words that can't be taken back.

Save me, O Lord, from a runaway tongue. Amen.

ANOTHER MINUTE
Read & meditate on Ephesians 4:29.

Set a guard, O LORD, over my mouth;
Keep watch over the door of my lips.
Psalm 141:3 NKJV

The Better Bone

A heart at peace gives life to the body,
but envy rots the bones.
—Proverbs 14:30 NIV

One morning I gave each of our dogs, Bobby and Charlie, a big, juicy venison bone before I sat down for my devotions.

There, I thought smugly as they settled on the living room carpet about six feet from each other, *that'll keep them quiet and occupied for a while.*

I sank down into the love seat and opened my Bible to the day's meditation. After a few minutes, Bobby got up, dropped his bone on the carpet at my feet, and stood over Charlie until she let go of hers. Quickly, he snapped it up and scooted behind the love seat. Charlie was too surprised to growl.

I didn't want a dog fight in the middle of my living room, so I picked up Bobby's bone and gave it to Charlie. It wasn't long before Bobby sneaked out from behind the love seat and, once again, snatched the bone Charlie was chomping on. I took the bone that Bobby had left and dropped it in front of Charlie. Catching on to Bobby's thievery, Charlie left the bone I gave her and went after Bobby's.

On and on the swapping went, each dog acting as though the other had the better bone. What I thought would make for peace, instead became a source of envy and caused trouble.

I, too, battle envy. When a friend drives by in a new vehicle, suddenly my trusty ten-year-old van looks rustier and rattles more loudly. After I've visited someone who has a nicer house than I have, it seems as though the furniture and the carpeting in my house have gotten shabbier overnight. And it's all too easy to find fault with those who I feel are smarter or more talented.

Like an acid, envy eats away at my peace of mind, my inner joy and contentment, and my relationships with others. No wonder God tells us to rid ourselves of envy (see 1 Peter 2:1). He knows what I'm still learning—that love, not envy, is the "better bone."

When I feel that tug of envy on my heart, O Lord, help me to be satisfied with what I have, for everything I have is a gift from You. Amen.

ANOTHER MINUTE

Read & meditate on 1 Peter 2:1-3.

A Good Work

He who began a good work in you will carry it on to completion until the day of Christ Jesus.

—Philippians 1:6 NIV

In 1911 my grandmother, then an eighteen-year-old Slovak girl, said good-bye to her parents for the last time. Until recently I never thought about how her parents must have felt, knowing they'd never see her again. But I'm sure they hoped Anna's life would reflect her upbringing.

Nearly a century later, my daughter, Anna's great-granddaughter, also sets her sights on distant horizons. I have mixed emotions—sadness, because a part of our lives is over; excitement, because a promising future lies before her; and anxiety, because I wonder if I've done the job right.

Does she have a value system that will help her in the tough decisions she'll inevitably have to make? Have I planted the seeds of a faith that will sustain her through the trying times that are sure to come? Have I given her a solid foundation?

As I look back over the years, I see the foundation blocks being laid, one layer at a time—praying together around the dinner table or during a crisis, rushing to get out the door to be on time for church and Sunday school, practicing for Christmas and Easter programs, preparing Good News Club lessons, packing up for a week at Camp Good News, picking up the neighborhood children for Vacation Bible School, driving four hours to Lancaster to bring her home after summer missionary training . . .

Although my foundation-building days are over, I know I am releasing my daughter to a Master Builder who will finish what He, not I, started.

Heavenly Father, be with my daughter as she makes her way in the world. Guide her in the problems she faces and in the decisions she makes. Amen.

ANOTHER MINUTE

Read & meditate on 1 Corinthians 3:6-11.

For no one can lay any foundation other than the one already laid, which is Jesus Christ.

1 Corinthians 3:11 NIV

Fish 'n Faith

"Put out into deep water, and let down the nets for a catch."

—Luke 5:4 NIV

I'm not crazy about fish, but I am crazy about my husband, so a few years ago we took a family vacation trip to Canada—to go fishing, of course. Terrified of deep water, I strapped on my life vest as tightly as I could and clung to the small boat as it roared across remote lakes or puttered through narrow channels. The tasty walleye we were after could only be found in deep water.

Because I can't swim, the fear of falling in was ever present. While others reeled in fish after fish, my line kept coming back empty—minus even the slimy minnows I'd managed to squish on the hook without throwing up. Eventually I did catch a "keeper," but only because I finally overcame my fear of drowning and listened to the directions of someone more experienced than me at fishing.

Letting go of fear and heeding someone wiser applies to more than fishing—it applies to my faith as well. There are times I doubt the Word of God. I just can't see the blessings He has promised in His Word if I will obey. Like Peter, I've "toiled all night and caught nothing" (Luke 5:5 NKJV). Rather than risk feeling insecure, I stay close to shore, wading only as far as my shallow faith will allow me. Yet He calls me to venture into the deep, yield my fears to Him, and open my heart to receive what He has for me.

Do I believe Him or don't I? If I choose to believe, then I need to risk going in over my head. If I choose not to believe, then I lose out on His blessings.

It didn't take a lot of faith for Peter to make the catch of a lifetime—just enough to turn the boat around. Neither do I need a lot of faith—just enough to venture out one more time.

Dear God, shore up my faltering faith. Amen.

Another Minute
Read & meditate on Luke 5:1-11.

Crutches

But let all who take refuge in you be glad;
let them ever sing for joy.
—Psalm 5:11 NIV

N*ow who brought those crutches down from the attic?* I wondered when I spied them leaning against the dining room wall. As far as I knew, everyone was walking without a limp, so off they went to the furnace room until I had the chance to take them back to the attic.

Although I pitch things that we no longer use, the crutches are good to have around. With kids who have been involved in ballet, cheerleading, track, wrestling, baseball, basketball, football, and soccer, the crutches have given numerous sprained ankles and knees time to heal. The injured joint is back to full power much more quickly if given time to rest. It makes no sense to limp around on a sprain and hinder both body movement and the healing process.

Sometimes our spirits suffer sprains, too. But rather than giving our wounds time to heal, we limp from day to day, wondering why we aren't recuperating more quickly. Perhaps we're too influenced by today's redneck image, which says, "I can handle this by myself. I don't need religion. It's just a crutch for those who aren't strong enough."

Well, *I* need a crutch when my spirit is wounded. I know I'm not tough enough to handle the hurt alone. I learned that, unless I lean on God, I just don't heal right.

We all lean on something when we hurt. Some of our crutches, such as alcohol, drugs, overeating, and yes, even chocolate, cause more harm than good. Others, such as exercise and prayer, give our overused, wounded spirits time to rest and to heal.

Mine is God. What's yours?

Thank You, Father, for letting me lean on You when I need rest and healing. You are the best crutch of all. Amen.

ANOTHER MINUTE

Read & meditate on Psalm 16.

Pockets

Let us turn away from everything wrong, whether of body or spirit, and purify ourselves, living in the wholesome fear of God, giving ourselves to him alone.
—2 Corinthians 7:1 TLB

I love pockets! Into them I cram the bits and pieces of my daily life—stuffing from the dog's chair, paper clips, pens, screws, fingernail clippers, gum wrappers, pop bottle caps, rubber bands, used and unusued tissues, receipts, keys, loose change, buttons, even the cat's shed hair.

One pocket is not enough. I like at least two. Into the left pocket I put the things I will throw away. Into the right pocket go the items I'll either use soon or need to put where they belong. At the end of the day I empty my pockets. It wouldn't do to carry today's debris around with me tomorrow, and neglecting to remove a tissue buried deep in the pocket of a pair of jeans that later get tossed into the washing machine can get messy. The items in my right pocket are put where they belong—in a cupboard, closet, or drawer. Tomorrow I will start my day with pockets clean and ready.

I have "spiritual" pockets, too. In them I stuff the bits and pieces of my spiritual life. Deep in my left pocket I push that exaggerated truth, twinge of envy, thoughtless remark, moment of discontent, act of selfishness, word of gossip, and bitter feelings. Into my right pocket go the things I often need at my fingertips: honesty, forgiveness, gratitude, compassion, kindness, gentleness, and humility.

Like my physical pockets, my spiritual ones also need to be emptied and scrutinized every day. Disposing each day of the accumulation in my left pocket through confession makes tomorrow's lighter to carry and quicker to discard. Too often, however, I don't dig deeply enough, and bits and pieces of an overlooked "tissue" cling to the fabric of my life. That's why it's important to ask God to show me what I've missed. After I've cleaned out my left pocket, I sort through the contents of my right pocket and apply them where they belong—to a relationship, attitude, habit, or perspective.

And tomorrow I start over, with pockets clean and ready.

Father God, keep Your hands in my pockets. Amen.

ANOTHER MINUTE
Read & meditate on Ephesians 4:23-32.

Red Flag Days

All your waves and breakers have swept over me.
—Psalm 42:7 NIV

When we went to Seaside Park on the Atlantic Coast one summer, I had visions of strolling through gently rolling waves lapping warm sands. How was I to know what those little yellow flags snapping in the stiff sea breeze meant? I sure found out when I tiptoed into the surf after my husband and son.

There was nothing gentle about the ocean that day. The only thing rolling was me! After getting pounded into the sand one too many times, I staggered to the safety and security of the blanket. *At least I got my sinuses cleaned out,* I thought, blowing my nose into a paper towel.

"What does that yellow flag mean?" I asked my husband when he dripped by.

"It means caution," he replied. "To be careful because the seas are a bit rough."

"NOW you tell me!" I choked.

"The green flag means calm seas, and the red flag danger. Usually you don't go out on a red flag day. That's when the waves are really high, but that's also when it's the best time to body surf."

Who wants to body surf? I thought. *I just want to romp in a gentle sea.*

I prefer the same as I live my life. I'd rather romp in gentle waves than endure the breakers on those red flag days. Then I have no choice but to plunge into the treacherous waves that sweep me off my feet and pound me into the surf. Reeling from onslaught after onslaught, I often wonder where God is while I'm being battered and beaten. But I needn't wonder too long. Just in time, he plucks me out of the raging seas and sets me down on the soft sands of His love. I realize then that, whether I'm in rough seas or on a sandy shore, He is always with me.

Thank You, Father, for being with me in the red flag days of my life. Amen.

ANOTHER MINUTE
Read & meditate on Psalm 42.

Why are you downcast, O my soul?
Why so disturbed within me?
Put your hope in God,
for I will yet praise him,
my Savior and my God.
Psalm 42:11 NIV

Travelin' Clothes

Do nothing out of selfish ambition or vain conceit.
—Philippians 2:3 NIV

I learned the value of dressing for the occasion years ago when my mother and I flew to Alabama to visit my brother, Pete, for Christmas. At twenty-one, I was on my own and proud of it. I wanted my appearance to reflect my self-image—a suave, savvy woman of the world. So for the trip, I wore a red velour mini-skirt with a matching short-waist, short-sleeved jacket, stockings, and dress shoes, which I have never found comfortable. I let my shoulder-length hair fall free, even though it had a mind of its own and usually ended up in my face. A black velvet choker necklace completed my travel attire.

Now, my mother was a simple woman quite naive in the ways of the world. Since my brother ate Southern cuisine and was "deprived" of the Slovak dishes we grew up on, she took it upon herself to take him a batch of homemade pierogies. You don't put a three-quart glass casserole dish filled to capacity with frozen food in the baggage compartment. You carry it on the airplane, hold it in your lap throughout the flight, and shiver.

I don't remember how I became the guardian of the goodies. Perhaps the image of my bird-like, aging mother lugging a lump of frost from Pittsburgh to Montgomery overcame the need to appear chic. It wouldn't have been so bad if we had taken a direct flight, and changing planes in Atlanta wouldn't have been as aerobic or traumatic if we wouldn't have had to change airlines.

Somewhere between Eastern and Delta I realized my carefully donned image was gone with the wind. *I would have been much more comfortable if I'd dressed simply in jeans and sneakers and tied my hair back,* I thought, feeling foolish, embarrassed, and immature. I'd been too concerned with how I appeared to others than with using common sense and dressing practically.

I've learned the same principle applies to our journey through life. Letting what others might think or say about us dictate how we talk, act, or dress only serves to slow us down and trip us up. But when we focus on "What will God think?" we find our progress is a lot smoother—even when we're carrying a batch of frozen pierogies.

Lord, show me those things that slow me down, hold me back, or trip me up spiritually. Help me to choose the right "traveling clothes." Amen.

ANOTHER MINUTE

Read & meditate on Hebrews 12:1-2.

Glow in the Dark

When Moses came down from Mount Sinai . . . his face was radiant because he had spoken with the LORD.
—Exodus 34:29 NIV

I can remember when I first discovered how glow-in-the-dark figures really worked. Until then I'd never really given much thought to how something could radiate light without being a source of light itself. I noticed how they shone brightly at first, then slowly lost their glow. Rather than give off light all by themselves, glow-in-the-dark figures radiate the light they've absorbed from a light source such as a light bulb or the sun. The brighter the light source and the closer and longer the exposure, the more light is absorbed and the brighter the glow.

I remember how I'd take a glow-in-the-dark figure and hold it close to a light bulb, then hurry to a darkened room so I could watch it glow. But the glow would eventually fade, and I'd have to return for more light.

Christians, too, are "glow-in-the-dark" figures. We are to radiate the light we absorb from God to a world darkened with selfishness and sin. The closer we get to Him and the longer we stay in His presence, the brighter we will glow.

I wonder how well I am radiating God to those around me. Too often I jump right into the day without taking much time to absorb His light through praying and reading His Word.

Then, when I go into the sin-darkened world, His radiance dims much too quickly.

Yes, I can go to church once or twice a week and catch some light, but it's only when I'm up close to God on a daily basis and spend adequate time with Him that I absorb—and then radiate—the most Light.

Remind me, O God, that my purpose in life is to radiate Your glory, for You alone are the true Source of Light. Amen.

ANOTHER MINUTE
Read & meditate on Matthew 5:14-16;
Exodus 34:29-35.

Minding My Mouth

Don't use foul or abusive language. Let everything you say be good and helpful, so that your words will be an encouragement to those who hear them.

—Ephesians 4:29 NLT

The aroma of home-fried potatoes browning in olive oil with sliced onions and crisp green peppers teased my nostrils as I lifted the lid of the cast iron skillet. *They'll be happy with supper tonight,* I thought, feeling rather pleased with myself. It wasn't often that I took the time to peel enough potatoes to satisfy my husband and my teenage son's appetites, which I liken to that of a bear right before hibernation time.

The potatoes turned out perfect, but the fried chipped ham, a favorite with my son, didn't. I kind of burned it trying to get it to brown right, and the cheap ketchup I added didn't darken as the more expensive brand did. *Would they notice?* I wondered.

"This tastes—different," my son commented as he chomped into his sandwich and forked the onions and peppers out of the potatoes on his plate.

"If you can't say anything positive, don't say anything at all," I shot at him, feeling put down.

"But all I said was it tastes different," he said. "I didn't say it was bad or anything."

"You didn't have to," I said, looking to my husband for

support. But he only grinned and said he was keeping his mouth shut.

"Thanks a lot," I spat at him. "You could at least stick up for me!"

Praise and appreciation around here are as extinct as the dinosaurs, I thought as we finished our meal in silence. *The food is always too hot, too cold, too spicy, too bland, too sweet, too bitter, or "different."*

Later that evening as I sat alone in my study, I wondered how often my own comments or even my silence might have hurt others. Do I tell my son how nice the lawn looks after he spends the day mowing and weed-eating? Or am I more concerned with the spots that he missed? Does my husband know how much I appreciate his dogged determination to fix things that I would have thrown out without a second thought? Or do I complain that I'd rather have something new?

I thought of all the little, everyday things that they do to make our lives run smoother. And here I was, pouting like a kid, more concerned with getting appreciation than giving it. Maybe it was time to start minding my mouth, too.

When I find myself about to criticize, please remind me, Lord, that praise goes a longer way. Amen.

ANOTHER MINUTE

Read & meditate on James 3:3-12.

Faces of Faith

For to see your face is like seeing the face of God.
—Genesis 33:10 NIV

I had to talk to someone before the fear rising in me erupted into a full-blown panic. My husband had been admitted to the hospital a few days earlier with a high fever and dangerously low blood pressure. Blood tests indicated the possibility of cancer. I'd always thought my faith would help me in times like this, but now I found I needed a real, live human being.

It was a Saturday afternoon, and nobody I knew within driving distance was home except a friend from church. I found Carl in his front yard, up to his knees in mud, digging up his septic system. I felt bad for bothering him, but being interrupted in the middle of a messy job didn't seem to annoy Carl. Instead, his face showed genuine concern. As I spilled out my fears and shed a few tears, I felt as though I was talking to Jesus Himself. Maybe it was the love I saw shining through Carl's eyes. I left comforted and fortified to face whatever lay ahead.

Although the indwelling Holy Spirit acts as our Comforter, there are times when we need the warm touch of another human being. A timely note, a gentle hug, a listening ear can do wonders to boost faith and hope.

Thankfully, my husband didn't have cancer. But I'll never forget when I saw the face of God in my friend Carl.

Dear Father, enable us to help others as we have been helped—to replace doubt with faith, despair with hope, and to comfort as we have been comforted. For it is through us that You reach a hurting world. Amen.

ANOTHER MINUTE

Read & meditate on John 17:20-26; Galatians 6:2.

Tuning Up

Direct my footsteps according to your word;
let no sin rule over me.
—Psalm 119:133 NIV

As an amateur musician, I've learned the importance of tuning my guitar each time I take it out of its case. Even one string out of tune creates discord, so I check each one carefully, using middle C on the piano as my guide. Only when I'm satisfied that all the strings are properly tuned and in harmony am I ready for my concert.

I, too, am an instrument that needs frequent tune-ups. And like the guitar, I must check each string separately.

First, I check the "E" string: How is my *enthusiasm*? Am I a wet blanket or a ray of sunshine? Do I maintain my initial gusto for a worthwhile project over the long haul? Do I approach each day and activity with eagerness and energy?

Next, I pluck the "B" string: Am I a *blessing* to those I meet daily? Do I uplift others not only in prayer but also by going out of my way to help in times of need? Do I encourage others when they face challenges that threaten to overwhelm them?

Next I check my *gratitude* level ("G"): Am I thankful for the good things that I have, or do I focus on what I don't have? Do I show my appreciation to others, or do I take it for granted that they should know I'm grateful? Is the phrase "thank you" part of my daily vocabulary?

On to the "D" string: Do I *discipline* myself to have a quiet time every day, to keep my mouth shut and think of the consequences of my words, to resist feelings of envy, to quell my anger, to use my time and resources wisely? Ah, that's a hard one. But it must be in tune before I check my *accountability* level ("A"): Do I accept responsibility for my thoughts, words, and actions? Do I make right that which I have done wrong, even when it's inconvenient or costs me time and money?

The bottom and final string is another "E." This one stands for *endurance*. Can I continue to do the right thing when I'm tired, hurting, or facing opposition? Do I keep plugging away and hang tight, or do I turn tail and run when the going gets tough? Do I choose to have faith and trust God before He answers my prayers?

And what do I use for my "middle C?" Jesus *Christ,* for all these others will be in tune only if I am in tune with Him.

Let my life be a pleasant song in Your ears, O Lord. Let my words and actions be in harmony with You. Amen.

ANOTHER MINUTE

Read & meditate on 1 John 1:3-5.

My Garden, My Life

I planted the seed, Apollos watered it,
but God made it grow.
—1 Corinthians 3:6 NIV

As a young girl growing up in a steel mill town 30 miles southeast of Pittsburgh, I dreamed of someday living in the country and eating fresh vegetables from my own garden. My dream came true—for awhile.

Our 75 by100 foot garden produced corn, beans, potatoes, carrots, lettuce, beets, onions, peppers, cucumbers, and tomatoes. Salads tasted crisp and sweet. Home-canned carrots and beans were just as fresh and flavorful in January as when they were first picked. The sparkling, colorful jars lining my pantry shelves filled me with as much pleasure as the first glimpse of tiny green shoots pushing up through soil we'd plowed, harrowed, fertilized, and seeded. Watching my garden grow each day, I felt a sense of accomplishment and pride and a oneness with nature and God.

Then the country critters found an easy feed, and I watched, heartbroken, as each year we harvested less and less. We tried fencing in the garden, hanging aluminum pie pans and human hair (which, we were told, would scare away the deer), setting box traps, and dusting bug repellent on the plants, but nothing worked. Exasperated, we finally gave up. It was easier to buy what we wanted at a farmer's market than to fight the forces of the forest. *Maybe it's better this way,* I told myself. *I need my time and energy for my family.* But deep down, I missed watching my garden grow.

As my children passed through their teen and young adult years, my garden lesson took on a new meaning. *You put your best effort into it,* I thought, *and something beyond your control comes and snatches away the harvest.* No matter that I went by "The Book." The bugs of rebellion and the blight of a morally bankrupt society crept in and threatened to destroy the fruit I'd so lovingly and painstakingly nurtured.

"Lord," I often prayed, "I'm doing my best, but my best isn't good enough. Help me."

Time and again, God showed me that He is, indeed, "able to do immeasurably more than all we ask or imagine" (Ephesians 3:20). My job is to shower them with love and prayer and trust Him to do the rest.

The past three years we've enjoyed fresh tomatoes from some plants next to the house. The critters either haven't found them or are too timid to venture near. But it doesn't matter because I've learned that even though we do the work, the results are in God's hands. And I can't think of any better hands than His.

When the results of my efforts don't turn out the way I want, remind me, Lord, that You are the one who makes my life's garden grow. Amen.

ANOTHER MINUTE

Read & meditate on 1 Corinthians 3:5-9.

Misleading Signs

"Tell us," they said, "when will this happen, and what will be the sign of your coming and of the end of the age?"
—Matthew 24:3 NIV

Spying the orange flags perched atop still another "Work Area Ahead" sign, I groaned inwardly.

"Can't I go anywhere anymore without running into road work?" I grumbled, slowing down slightly. It wouldn't have mattered so much if I hadn't been running fifteen minutes late, as usual.

I passed two more signs warning me of a "flagman ahead" and that I'd better "be prepared to stop." I sighed, mentally practicing my excuse for being late.

As I drove farther down the road, however, it became apparent the road crews weren't working, at least not yet. I'd noticed on occasion "work area" signs along the road, but no crew working. I never knew when to believe the signs and when not to. This time I decided not to. Pushing down on the gas pedal, I sped around a curve. Just then a speck of orange up ahead caught my eye. Braking staccato, I was able to stop without making a fool of myself or killing the flagman.

"When are you going to learn to heed the signs?" I scolded myself.

"It's always better to be ready than to be caught

unprepared." That's what Jesus told His disciples when they asked Him about the end of the world.

"Watch out no one deceives you," He warned them. "Keep watch, because you do not know on what day your Lord will come. So you also must be ready, because the Son of Man will come at an hour when you do not expect him" (Matthew 24:4, 42, 44 NIV).

Today, too many people have been fooled by false signs. Self-proclaimed "prophets" try to pinpoint Jesus' return. But Jesus warned about them and instructed His followers to watch and be ready (see Matthew 24:42-44). It really doesn't matter who believes what about the "when" and the "how" of His return. What does matter is that we believe He *will* return and are ready for His coming, whether it's down the road or around the next bend.

Let me not put too much emphasis on trying to interpret the signs of the times, Lord Jesus. Rather let me focus on living my life so that I am always ready for Your return. Amen.

ANOTHER MINUTE

Read & meditate on Matthew 24.

Calling Home

My soul thirsts for God.
—Psalm 42:2 NKJV

I wasn't home one Friday evening when my daughter, Jaime, called from Montana where she was attending school the summer after she graduated from high school. I hadn't seen her for nearly a month and had been looking forward to her weekly call. While I was glad her dad got to spend some time talking on the phone with her, I was disappointed that I'd missed what was becoming one of the brighter spots of my week.

"Oh, well," I sighed. "There's always next week."

When the phone rang Monday evening, I wasn't expecting it to be Jaime, so I was pleasantly surprised when I heard her voice.

She missed me Friday and called just to talk to me. I thought.

After some small talk, she got down to why she was calling.

"Can you send me $35?" she asked.

I really should have known better, but my heart rules my head sometimes, especially when it comes to those I love. I want to be as important to her as she is to me, but she's young and trying her wings for the first time. Although I want her to fly, I'd still like to hear the words, "Mom, I love you, and I miss you. I called just to hear your voice."

Am I not guilty of the same attitude when it comes to

talking to God? I rush through my devotions, checking off each page of my devotional booklets like a "to-do" list, keeping my eye on the clock all the while. I rattle off requests and tack on "in Jesus' name" at the end, feeling as though I've done my duty for the day.

Oh, I know God wants me to bring my needs to Him and that He knows what they are before I even ask. But how much more precious in His eyes are the times I come to Him with no special request—the times when all I want is to hear His voice.

Father, I love You, and I miss You when I rush through my quiet time. Today I have no special requests—I only want to hear Your voice and bask in Your presence. Amen.

ANOTHER MINUTE

Read & meditate on Mark 1:35; Psalm 42:1-2.

Still Pluggin' Away

"My grace is sufficient for you, for my power is made perfect in weakness."

—2 Corinthians 12:9 NIV

After only nine years, my vacuum cleaner looks like it's been through World War II. The switch doesn't work, so whenever I want to shut it off, I have to unplug it. No longer does it glide gracefully across the floor. Someone dropped it, driving the front wheel through the plastic casing on the bottom. To get more suction, I pulled off the wheel and taped bread bags over the hole, inside and out. For good measure, I wrapped duct tape across the bottom of the canister.

One of the tubes is a replacement from my husband's spare parts pile. Duct tape covers air leaks in the hose. The pulley for the power cord is broken. The lights don't work, and the upholstery brush keeps falling off.

Perhaps by now frustration would have driven someone else to buy a new machine. Not me. In spite of all that's wrong with it, my vacuum cleaner is still doing what it was made to do—suck up dirt, dust, and debris.

I'm a lot like that vacuum cleaner. I, too, have parts that don't work as well as they used to, and I don't get around as gracefully as I once did. Occasionally someone has to pull my plug before I burn myself out, and sometimes I need extra parts to hold me together. But, as God reminds me in His Word, those aren't excuses to avoid doing what He's created me to do.

I know of an elderly couple who served as missionaries in Alaska despite declining health. Helen, a writer, still composed devotionals on her deathbed, dictating her thoughts to her daughter, who submitted them to the local newspaper.

My friend, Dorothy, continued to teach her Sunday school class in spite of temporary blindness in one eye.

God promises us the strength to do the job He's given us to do. So, with His power, I'm just going to keep pluggin' away.

Dear God, thank You for my weaknesses, for it is through them that others can see You at work in my life. Amen.

ANOTHER MINUTE

Read & meditate on 2 Corinthians 12:5-10.

Praise Page

A cheerful heart is good medicine,
but a crushed spirit dries up the bones.
—Proverbs 17:22 NIV

It was definitely one of the lowest times in my life. Everything that meant anything to me seemed to be slipping away. I'd worked hard and sacrificed to do the right thing, but what did I have to show for it? Where were my rewards? No matter how hard I tried to make things better, "one step forward, ten steps backward" pretty much described my life. Was this middle age crisis? If so, I'd never joke about it again.

Even my prayer time had degenerated into a grumbling session. No wonder it seemed as though God had gone deaf as far as I was concerned. Who wanted to listen to a litany of woes?

"Lord," I asked one morning, "what am I to do?"

Philippians 4:6 (NIV)came to mind immediately: "Do not be anxious about anything, but in everything, by prayer and petition, *with thanksgiving*, present your requests to God" [emphasis added].

Okay, I thought, *I'll give it a try.* Opening my journal, I began to list all that I could praise God for: A loving, faithful, loyal, steadfast, hard-working husband who puts up with my moods and goes along with all my plans. My kids, who never fail to hug me and tell me they love me. My best friend, Sharon, who always takes time for me and says just what I need to hear. Good health. A house in the country. A good well. My husband's job, which provides steady work and a regular income. Part-time job opportunities doing what I enjoy most—teaching and writing—that still allow time for my family.

On and on I wrote. Praises gushed out like water from a well that's been primed. I felt the heaviness begin to lift. Right then I resolved to list every day just one thing for which I'm thankful. Although I haven't kept my "praise page" as I'd planned, when I'm down in the dumps again, I know it's time to give life a lift with praise.

When I'm ready to complain, Lord, remind me of something for which I'm thankful. Amen.

ANOTHER MINUTE
Read & meditate on Philippians 4:4-8.

Why are you downcast, O my soul?
Why so disturbed within me?
Put your hope in God,
for I will yet praise him, my Savior and God.
Psalm 42:11 NIV

Slow Leak

If we confess our sins, He is faithful and just to forgive us our sins and to cleanse us from all unrighteousness.
—1 John 1:9 NKJV

"Keep an eye on that left front tire," my husband told me. "It has a slow leak."

I groaned. Around our place, broken things usually don't get fixed right away, so that slow leak meant I would have to check the tire every time I used my car. If too much air escaped and I drove on a low tire, it would be ruined. So I kept an eye on it—for awhile. But life has a way of getting busy, and little things, such as checking the tire, sometimes go by the wayside—until, of course, the tire goes flat, and I'm stranded by the highway, trying to figure out how the jack works. That's when I hope for a Good Samaritan to come along and change the tire for me. It's a lot easier, though, to find the leak and fix it *before* I get stranded and ruin the tire.

Tires aren't the only things that develop slow leaks. Our spirits do, too. After filling up on God's Word, I head into my day filled with good intentions. But too often, "slow leaks" develop. Not only do I listen to gossip, I also justify it by telling myself I'm being a good listener. Then my mouth gets into the act, and suddenly that slow leak gets a bit faster. I also lose air when I envy others, when I'm not satisfied with what I have, or when I let pride become a motivating force for my actions.

Simply filling up my spiritual tires, however, isn't enough. I need to find the leaks and seal them, or my witness will be ruined. Finding them is as simple as asking God to reveal them to me. Then I seal them by confessing to God all those wrong thoughts, attitudes, and actions and asking Him for the strength to resist (see 1 Corinthians 10:13 and James 4:7)

We all develop slow leaks. It's watching for them daily and fixing them right away that makes traveling life's road a whole lot smoother.

Search me, O God, and know my heart; test me and know my thoughts. See if there is any offensive way in me, and lead me in the way everlasting. Create in me a clean heart. Amen. *

ANOTHER MINUTE
Read & meditate on Matthew 15:1-20.

*See Psalm 139:23-24; 51:10. Praying the Scriptures is an exciting way to deepen your prayer life.

Morning Prayer

When I consider your heavens,
the work of your fingers, the moon and the stars,
which you have set in place,
what is man that you are mindful of him,
the son of man that you care for him?
—Psalm 8:3 NIV

Good morning, Lord. Thank You for the beautiful sunrise. Thank You that I got up early enough to see the orange glow that streaked across the sky as I emptied the dishwasher and waited for the water to boil for my tea.

Thank You that I didn't hobble around this morning like I usually do when I get out of bed. I actually feel as though I got a good night's sleep, even though I woke up every two hours. Thank You that my nocturnal aches and pains didn't keep me wrestling with the covers all night, preventing my husband from getting the rest he needs.

Thank You, Lord, for this wonderful cup of tea I sip in the hush before the world awakens. This morning's sky is still another reminder that You are with me constantly. Nature has always brought me a renewed sense of Your presence.

Please walk with me, Lord, into this brand new day that stretches before me like a field of unbroken snow. Let the tracks I make head in the direction You would have me to go. Place

Your desires in my heart so that I want what You want.

Open my eyes to the needs around me. Help me to see beneath the masks, to feel the pain beneath the armor, and to respond as Jesus would. And when someone says or does something that offends me, remind me, Lord, of all those who overlook my faults and offenses. Help me to be patient with others as You are with me.

Guide me in the problems I will face and in the decisions I must make. Protect my loved ones and provide for our needs. Draw us closer to each other and to You, Lord, for You are what we need most. Let us never forget that. Help me to be the wife my husband needs and the mother my children need.

Grant me Your wisdom, for mine is so inadequate. Clear away the static of a thousand conflicting voices—all of which profess wisdom—so that I hear Your voice, loud and clear.

And now, Lord, it's time to rinse my empty cup, say "Amen," and tackle that ambitious "Do List." Help me not to feel like a failure when I don't get everything done. And please help me to welcome interruptions as opportunities to serve You.

And when I slip into bed tonight with a cup of "Sweet Dreams" tea in one hand and the day's newspaper in the other, let me hear Your voice whispering, "Well done, good and faithful servant." Amen.

ANOTHER MINUTE

Read & meditate on Psalm 8.

No More Night

There will be no more night . . . for the Lord God will give them light.

—Revelation 22:5 NIV

When my mother-in-law was diagnosed with advanced lung cancer in December 1998, we knew the prognosis was not good. Even so, we hoped the proposed treatments would buy her enough time to see two of her grandchildren get married the following summer. One week into her treatments, however, she died suddenly, leaving us stunned.

In the days that followed, I avoided looking at her house, about fifty yards from mine, when I turned the corner of the driveway. The darkened windows were a painful reminder that she was no longer there to turn on the lights against the coming night. I hadn't realized how much seeing those lights had meant to me.

Then one evening my husband left a lamp on in her living room. What a comfort! The house didn't seem so empty or forlorn. Although I knew she wasn't there, that single light shining in the darkness somehow gave my grieving heart hope.

"I don't think of Grandma as dead," my youngest commented the day after her death. "I think of her as in a better place."

The Apostle John tells us a little about this "better place" in

Revelation: "God himself will be with them and be their God. He will wipe away every tear from their eyes. There will be no more death or mourning or crying or pain. . . . There will be no more night. They will not need the light of a lamp or the light of the sun, for the Lord God will give them light" (21:3,4; 22:5 NIV).

Night is the time we feel the grief most deeply. Its very blackness screams hopelessness. But God's Son, Jesus Christ, conquered night. Through His death and resurrection, He has given us the hope of eternal day.

When the night closes in on me, O Lord, remind me that with Jesus, there truly is no more night—only eternal light and life. Amen.

ANOTHER MINUTE

Read & meditate on Revelation 21:1-5; 22:1-6.

Pop 'n' Stop

"Come to me, all you who are weary and burdened, and I will give you rest."

—Matthew 11:28 NIV

On a dusty bookshelf in my cluttered study is a glass jar with exactly 1,440 kernels of popcorn, each representing one minute of the day. I put the jar there a few years ago as a reminder not to waste my time—that each minute of every day is precious and should be used wisely.

Those were the days I listened to motivational speakers and writers who urged me to produce and achieve, using catchy slogans easy to remember. Even Bible verses seemed to promise me success if I only believed. It all sounded so simple: Just dream it, believe it, plan it, work 'til you drop, and *Voila!* Those dreams would come true.

So I dreamed, planned, worked hard, believed, and tried to cram every minute of every day with activities that would help me achieve my goals. But all that only served to make me feel guilty for not winning the Pulitzer Prize for my writing or being named "Someone of the Year." Even when I took a Sunday afternoon nap, I'd wake up and think of what I could have done if I hadn't slept.

I no longer took time for activities that once brought pleasure and relaxation, such as playing Scrabble with my son, visiting with a friend, watching the sun set, reading a good book, or immersing myself in music. When I was at work, I'd feel guilty for not being at home, taking care of my family. When I took time off to spend some time at home, I'd feel guilty for not working and helping to make ends meet. No matter what I did, I felt guilty.

A physician once told me, "As Americans we live terrible lifestyles. We don't sleep right. We tend to work too much and not eat right. We tend to waste our energy."

God didn't create us to be work machines. Nor does He want us to do nothing. Even Adam and Eve had a garden to tend. A healthy lifestyle balances work with rest.

My jar of popcorn still reminds me to use my time wisely—but wisely means knowing when to pop and when to stop.

Give me wisdom, O Lord, to balance my day with work and rest. Amen.

ANOTHER MINUTE
Read & meditate on Exodus 20:8-11.

When There's Nothing Left

"You will seek me and find me when you search for me with all your heart."

—Jeremiah 29:13 NIV

Kneeling beside my husband in the cool, pre-dawn darkness, I felt as though my whole life was coming apart at the seams. Everything that meant anything to me seemed to be slipping away. After twenty-three years of marriage, I felt as though my husband and I were drifting further and further apart. My three children were all at difficult stages, and at times I questioned sacrificing my career twenty years earlier to stay home and raise them. Years of living on the edge financially were taking their toll. In addition, I'd recently determined it was time to leave the church where we'd made so many cherished friendships over sixteen years.

Lost on a sea of emotional pain, I needed to get away. The morning before I was to fly to Alabama to visit my brother, I asked my husband to pray with me. With my arms around him, I knelt on the carpet in the darkened living room and visualized carrying my heartache, like a wounded, broken bird, to my heavenly Father.

"Lord," I cried silently, "I've done my best, but it just keeps getting worse. Make it better. Please. I give it all to You—no strings attached. I don't know what else to do."

When I flew out of Pittsburgh the next day, I honestly didn't know if I'd return. I was that burned out. The next nine days I spent on my knees—and, yes, even on my face—in prayer. Stripped of everything that I thought was important, and left with only God, I discovered God—finally. Then He began putting the broken pieces of me back together.

Today my marriage is stronger, my husband is growing spiritually, my children bring me more joy than I ever dreamed, and we've found another church to call home. Finances are getting back under control.

But it took nearly losing everything to find that "everything" is really God.

Thank You, Father, for meeting me in my time of deepest need. Amen.

ANOTHER MINUTE
Read & meditate on Psalm 57.

I will take refuge in the shadow of your wings
until the disaster has passed.
Psalm 57:1 NIV

The Melon and Me

"I am the vine; you are the branches. . . . apart from me you can do nothing."

—John 15:5 NIV

When I cut into the watermelon, my hopes for a cool, refreshing Fourth of July dessert vanished. The inside was almost white.

"And I thought it sounded hollow," I lamented, recalling tapping several melons that were in the bin at the supermarket. Too late now. If I wanted watermelon, I'd have to eat it unripened.

Is it that I simply don't know how to pick a good melon, or are growers picking them from the vines before they have a chance to ripen? It seems a good bit of the produce I buy these days lacks the flavor I remember in the fruits and vegetables we grew in our garden a few years ago.

"Melons, cucumbers, tomatoes—everything seems so bland anymore," I complained to my husband. "I guess today profit comes before quality."

Vines provide the fruit with the nourishment it cannot get on its own. The roots of the vine reach down into the soil for water and nutrients. Its leaves absorb sunlight and moisture. Apart from the vine, the immature fruit will never achieve its full potential. It might look ripe, even tasty, but it will lack the flavor of fruit that has remained on the vine.

I need to remember the lesson of the vine when I get too rushed to take time soaking up the nourishment I get from spending time with God. Feeling pressure to get more and more done, I sit down to write, but the words don't come. When I do manage to wring out a few feeble phrases from my stalled brain, they don't seem to have any punch.

On the other hand, when I've taken the time to read Scripture, meditate, and pray, the words and ideas seem to flow. How much better a piece is when I've paused to pray, "Lord, what do You want me to write? Show me how You want this done. Write this piece through me."

I guess the melon and I have something in common: We both need the Vine.

Lord, remind me today that without You, I can do nothing. Amen.

ANOTHER MINUTE

Read & meditate on John 15:1-6.

On Angels' Wings

For he will give his angels charge over you
to keep you in all your ways.
—Psalm 91:11 NKJV

Chills ran through me as I gaped at the demolished car. All four tires were flat, the windshield shattered, the roof crushed. While driving her boyfriend Robert's car, my daughter, Jaime, had taken a downhill curve on a gravel road too fast and lost control. The compact plunged down an embankment and slammed into a huge rock, finally settling on its roof—on top of Robert, who'd been ejected.

An emergency medical helicopter rushed Robert to the nearest trauma center, where medical personnel feared a crushed chest, two broken legs, and internal injuries. Yet twenty-four hours later he walked out of the hospital with eight stitches and a few bumps and bruises. Jaime, who'd been thrown around inside the car, escaped with bruises and lacerations.

I don't believe they were merely "lucky." Nearly two weeks before the accident, I'd felt a growing burden for Jaime during the Sunday morning worship service at our church. I closed my eyes and started to pray. As we sang "He is Able," I felt an overwhelming sense of God's presence. Love, light, and warmth enveloped me and Jaime, who stood beside me.

She's going to be all right; I have her in My hands. The words weren't spoken audibly, yet I heard them in my heart. A week later I had the urge to collar everyone I met and ask them to pray for my daughter. The day of the accident, Robert's name popped into my mind during my prayer time. Coincidence?

I pray daily for God to give His angels charge over my family, to keep them in all their ways. When the car slammed into the rock, the impact created a diagonal dent in the roof just big enough for a small, eighteen-year-old boy to fit in. Robert was lying in the dent.

Thank You, God, for Your ministering angels. Thank You for protecting me and those I love. Amen.

ANOTHER MINUTE

Read & meditate on Psalm 91.

Up and Away

If I take the wings of the morning,
and dwell in the uttermost parts of the sea;
Even there thy hand shall lead me,
and thy right hand shall hold me.
—Psalm 139:9-10 KJV

As my oldest son moved through his sometimes tumultuous high school years, I'd jokingly threaten to hang a huge banner on the front of the house when we had his graduation party: *Good-bye, good luck, good riddance!*

Then graduation day came all too soon. Two days later he left home for the first time, taking a job on a drilling rig that left early Monday morning and didn't return until late Friday.

The house was almost too quiet now. No one picked up the youngest, turned him upside-down, and shook him until he squalled. No one teased the dog so much she scrambled crazily around the living room, growling and yapping. No one devoured nearly half the mashed potatoes almost as soon as the bowl hit the table. No one barged into the bedroom at night as I was falling asleep to say, "I love you, Mom. You mean a lot to me."

The time had come. The nest was beginning to empty. For all my bravado, I really wasn't ready for it. Then I found myself humming an old song on Monday mornings as I drove him to work: "*Vaya Con Dios*"—"Go with God." Of course! God would be with him wherever he went, in whatever he did. My children are God's children, too.

Thank You, Father, for my children and the assurance that You love them even more than I do. Amen.

ANOTHER MINUTE
Read & meditate on Isaiah 43:1-7.

"I" Trouble

perception
fuzzy
can't see too far ahead
headaches
from "I" strain
use my "I's" too much
without
the right light

need to
give my "I's" a rest
see the world
through the lens
of selflessness
and
in the light of
God's Word.

An Appointment with Myself

There is a time for everything,
and a season for every activity under heaven.
—Ecclesiastes 3:1 NIV

Working at the appointments' desk at a writers' conference, I was responsible for setting up appointments for conferees with editors and published authors whom they hoped could help them in their quest for publication. With nearly 300 attending, things got hectic at times. When one author came to check for changes on his schedule, I realized I'd goofed. I'd written the name of the author instead of the conferee in the 4:00 P.M. slot for that day.

"Hey, Bob," I quipped, "you have an appointment with yourself at 4:00."

"Great!" he replied with a grin. "I always like talking to myself."

We all laughed, but it got me thinking. Maybe that's something I need to do occasionally—make an appointment with myself.

In the daily rush to get everything done, I keep waiting for life to settle down. I almost envy the folks I see sitting leisurely on their front porches while I whiz by. My "times of refreshing" are all too few.

But maybe that's my fault. I forget that I'm the one who really sets my schedule. Sure, things come up that are beyond my control, but there's a lot more that is within my control. In my struggle to be all things to and do all things for everyone, I end up frazzled and out of touch with myself.

The Old Testament tells us that God "blessed the seventh day and made it holy, because on it he rested from all the work of creating that he had done" (Genesis 2:3 NIV).

Now, God is the source of all energy. He doesn't need to rest, as we know it. But He knew we need times to be refreshed, renewed, and reacquainted with who we are, so He set the example for us.

Spending time with myself doesn't mean I'm selfishly neglecting work that is mine to do. On the contrary, when I emerge from my appointment with myself, I find my energy renewed, my spirit refreshed, and my identity restored. Then I can better do the work He has put me on earth to do.

When I get too busy, Lord, remind me there's a time for everything—even a time out for me. Amen.

ANOTHER MINUTE

Read & meditate on Ecclesiastes 3:1-15.

The Great Grumbler

Do everything without complaining.
—Philippians 2:14 NIV

Every pair of windshield wipers we get for our van, it seems, can't get the job done quietly. Rather than listen to that irritating scrape-scrape, scrape-scrape every time it rains, I find myself driving down the road peering through a blurry windshield, flicking on the wipers only when I absolutely have to.

I, too, can make a lot of noise doing something I'm supposed to be doing but that I don't particularly like. I clamor and complain, gripe and grumble, murmur and mutter while I'm scrubbing the bathroom, mopping the floor, or cleaning the kitchen. I show my displeasure in other ways, too. I'm great at slamming doors and drawers. Or giving my husband and kids "The Look." It really doesn't make the job any easier. In fact, when I've completed my task, I almost feel guilty for making such a big deal out of it.

On the way to the Promised Land, after being freed from the slavery of Egypt, the Israelites grumbled every step of the way—even after God performed miracle after miracle for them. They were hungry; God gave them manna. They got bored with manna; God gave them quail. They were thirsty; God gave them water from a rock in the middle of the desert. Then, when they got to the "land flowing with milk and honey," they complained that the natives were too big to fight. Their grumbling showed a lack of trust in a God who proved over and over that He'd take care of them. Rather than see the blessings, they focused on their own lack, forgetting God's power to provide.

I, too, need to remember that gratitude, not grumbling, makes the job—and the journey—a lot smoother.

Give me an attitude of gratitude, O God, so that my grumbling will cease. Amen.

ANOTHER MINUTE
Read & meditate on Exodus 15:22—17:7.

May the words of my mouth
and the meditation of my heart
be pleasing in your sight,
O LORD, my Rock and my Redeemer.
Psalm 19:14 NIV

Welcome to the World

Every good and perfect gift is from above, coming down from the Father . . .

—James 1:17 NIV

The sky glowed golden at sunset the day before you were born. A little after three in the morning your Aunt Jaime announced from the bedroom doorway, "The baby's on its way! The baby's on its way!" When I called the hospital four hours later, your mommy told me you had arrived.

Brent Michael Huey. Our first grandchild. Seven pounds, six ounces of pure joy. I'd forgotten. Life has a way of throwing enough curve balls that we forget what it's really all about. I'd built a wall around my heart to shut out the disappointments, grief, frustrations—all the pain that living in this world brings. But that wall also shut out the joy and the love. Oh, I smiled and said I was doing "good," even "great," when people asked how I was. But in reality, deep down inside, I felt little emotion.

When I knew you were here, Brent, that old wall just crumbled. Just your name is enough to bring tears of joy. But, oh, when I saw you! When I held you for the first time, you never even woke up for the whole hour and a half. As you slept soundly, I gently rocked you in my lap, one hand supporting your floppy little neck and the other beneath the blanketed bundle of you.

As I watched all those little baby faces you made, I dreamed of sitting in the rocker with you on my lap and reading to you; of walking with your little hand in mine and showing you all the wonders of God's creation—a rainbow, a sunset, a snowflake; of feeling your little arms around my neck and inhaling your sweet baby smell. The Big Dipper isn't big enough to contain the love I feel when I look at you!

Maybe that's why God painted the sky golden the evening before you entered my world—to remind me where life's treasures really are—that they are not in how well I write, how much money I have in the bank, how many awards I've collected, how clean my house is, or how little I weigh. Life, my little grandson, is loving and giving and caring and sharing—and stopping by the roadside to enjoy a golden sunset.

Welcome to the world, Baby Huey.

Thank You, God, for this little child—bone of my bone and flesh of my flesh—who has reawakened love and joy in my life-beaten heart. Amen.

ANOTHER MINUTE

Read & meditate on Psalm 139:13-18.

One Chair At a Time

We are the clay, you are the potter;
we are all the work of your hand.
—Isaiah 64:8 NIV

What I can only describe as "gunk" coated my once beautiful dining room chairs—right where grubby, greasy little fingers had grasped the finished pine. Scratches etched the seats and dried milk spotted the rungs where two teething puppies had soothed their gums. A vinyl tablecloth hid pockmarks made when hungry toddlers had used silverware as drumsticks.

"Someday I'm going to refinish this set," I promised myself time and again over the years. But the plan to get it done all at one time simply wasn't practical for a family of five. Then one morning after breakfast, I impulsively grabbed a bottle of ammonia and a rag and began rubbing. To my amazement, the sticky black goo came right off, along with the varnish I'd polished weekly in my pre-parent days. Half an hour later, I inspected my work. The chair still looked unsightly, but now could be sanded, stained, and refinished.

If I did one chair a week, I reasoned, I'd have the whole set done in less than two months. Broken down into smaller steps, the job I once thought overwhelming now seemed possible.

God works with me the same way. When I became a Christian, I thought God would make me over all at once (see 2

Corinthians 5:17) and I'd instantly be a perfect specimen of Christianity. Then I'd trip over my own faults and think I wasn't being changed at all. But like my dining room furniture, it takes time to remove the black goo of sin's residue that sticks to my soul. As I look back over the years, I see where God *has* been making me over—one "chair" at a time.

Thank You, Father, for Your transforming hand on my life. Amen.

ANOTHER MINUTE

Read & meditate on Jeremiah 18:1-4.

Just Trippin' Along

If the LORD delights in a man's way,
he makes his steps firm.
—Psalm 37:23 NIV

No sooner had my husband hooked up the new hot water heater, than I noticed the soapy water on the floor around the clothes washer.

"Please tell me it's the hose leaking," I said to my husband. Instead he gave me that you-know-our-luck look and shook his head. Although I've used this particular washing machine for nearly twenty-four years, the expense of buying a new one would blow the budget right out of the water. Besides, I could think of a dozen other ways I'd rather spend the money—such as carpeting for my study or a roof over the patio.

After mopping up the mess with old towels, we ignored the problem for a couple of days. Maybe the next time I used the washer, the floor would remain dry.

Three days later, our ignore-it-and-it-might-go-away plan seemed to be working. That is, until I noticed little black specks of grease on the load of whites. I rinsed that load again, shoved it into the dryer, shut the door, and pushed the start button. With each revolution, the dryer emitted a loud, grinding noise.

So I hung the load on the line outside. A nice breeze was blowing, and the sky was clearing after an early morning storm. *That should do it,* I thought, returning to my computer. An hour later I heard rain beating against my study window.

Sometimes one thing after another goes wrong, even as we try to live our lives in obedience to God's Word. But obedience doesn't make us immune from the troubles that are a normal part of life. There was a time when I whined to God every time a problem, big or small, tripped me up. But no more. Each one I encounter drives home the lesson that God doesn't promise us a road unmarked by difficulties. What He does promise, though, is that He will be with us every step of the way.

Father, sometimes I really don't want to walk the road I see before me. Grant me an increasing sense of Your nearness with every step I take. Amen.

ANOTHER MINUTE
Read & meditate on Romans 5:1-5.

The Peach Tree and Me

This plan of mine is not what you would work out, neither are my thoughts the same as yours! For just as the heavens are higher than the earth, so are my ways higher than yours, and my thoughts than yours.

—Isaiah 55:8-9 TLB

It's a sight I thought I'd never see: Peaches—red, yellow, orange—dotting the shaggy August grass beneath the tree in our yard. One branch is so laden that the entire tree arches to the ground. In my kitchen the fuzzy fruit fills a stainless steel bowl, attracting both hungry hands and fruit flies. Even after giving some away, I have enough to make a pie. And still more fruit is ripening on the tree I once thought dead.

Shortly after we moved to the country, I'd ordered a half dozen fruit trees from a seed catalog. We'd planted the six-inch seedlings when they arrived, looking limp and lifeless after being shipped halfway across the country. The apple and pear trees took root and grew, but the peach trees shriveled and died. So it seemed.

Then one day two or three years later, I noticed a tiny shoot pushing up through the spring ground. I dared not get my hopes up. The odds of fresh peach pie from my own peaches were low. So I thought.

The stubborn seedling, however, persisted through summer storms, winter winds, foraging wildlife, my son's mowing, and my indifference.

Even if the tree makes it, I thought, *we won't get any fruit because we need two trees for pollination.* But one year small balls of green fuzz appeared on the tree. *They won't be any good,* I thought. *They'll stay small and deformed because we neither spray nor fertilize them.*

Now, nearly nineteen years after planting it, the peach tree is at last fruitful. I think I knew all along that God was using that tree to teach me an important lesson. Back then, I, too, was a seedling when it came to matters of faith. I wanted to see the results of my efforts right away; God wanted me to believe He was working even when I couldn't see a situation changing for the better. I wanted my prayers answered my way; God wanted me to trust Him for the best answer, even if it wasn't what I prayed for. I wanted immediate answers to my prayers; God wanted me to learn to wait on Him and to know that His timing is always best.

I didn't understand then why God didn't answer my prayers. But, just like the peach tree was growing underground, God was working unseen in my life, growing the fruit He knew would last.

The fruit of the Spirit is love, joy, peace, patience, kindness, goodness, faithfulness, gentleness and self-control (Galatians 5:22 NIV). O Lord, grow Your fruit in my life! Amen.

ANOTHER MINUTE

Read & meditate on Isaiah 55:8-13.

Water Them Well

"But whoever drinks the water I give him will never thirst."

—John 4:14 NIV

Summer's heat and humidity can suck the life out of every living thing in sight. The grass, brown and dry, crunches underfoot. Physical movements are limited as we try to keep from sweating too much. Fans blast warm air through stuffy rooms. Even the dog seeks a cool refuge. The basement is popular with both man and beast.

In the evenings after supper, I fill plastic gallon jugs with water to pour over my poor, wilting flowers. I've finally learned to water them well. Once I neglected them for a few days and thought I'd lost them. Instead of two gallons, I give them six.

Life can be like that. The heat and humidity of daily struggles can suck the joy right out of us—a job layoff, an unforeseen expense we can't afford, concern over a sick or wayward child. All these can leave our spirits drooping and thirsty.

We, too, must be watered daily. Our water comes not from plastic gallon jugs but from the Source of life itself. That Source will never run dry. I must remember to water myself daily with prayer and Bible reading and make sure enough is poured so my spirit will not droop amidst the heat and humidity of life.

Lord, remind me to water myself frequently and well with the Word of Life so I will not wilt when trials come to dry my soul. Amen.

ANOTHER MINUTE
Read & meditate on John 4:5-14.

Thanksgiving

I'm thankful for the muddy floor
that greets me every day;
I'm thankful for the dirty socks
that on the floor doth lay.
I'm thankful for the fingerprints
that deck both chair and wall.
I'm thankful for the daily dust
that on the desk doth fall.
I'm thankful for the toothpaste
smeared on the bathroom door;
I'm thankful for the wad of gum
stuck to the kitchen floor.
I'm thankful for the scattered toys
that often pierce my feet
when I must run to get the phone
before I've time to sweep.
I'm thankful for the mending
I love so much to do
That I hide it in the corner
and buy them something new.
I'm thankful for the unmade beds
that mean I'm not alone;
I'm thankful for so many things
that make our house a home.

No Fear

I sought the LORD *and he answered me;*
he delivered me from all my fears.
—Psalm 34:4 NIV

We are about ready to fall asleep when the phone rings. It is my nineteen-year-old daughter in Kansas, 1,700 miles away.

"Mom? What should I do? The building across the street from my apartment is burning down."

"Which way is the wind blowing?" I ask.

"This way. My apartment is filled with smoke. I have all my favorite clothes packed in my biggest suitcase. I'm surprised I haven't been evacuated yet."

"Make sure you pack all your important papers," I say, surprisingly calm.

"I packed them," she says. "Just a minute. Someone's at the door."

I wait.

"Mom? That was the fireman. He said I didn't have to, but it would be wise to evacuate. Boy, was he cute! Well, I'd better get going."

"Where will you go?" I ask.

"I have some friends who I can stay with."

"Be careful, sweetheart," I say. "I love you."

"I love you, too," she answers before hanging up.

Still I feel no fear. The next morning, after a restful sleep, I call her apartment. I figure if the answering machine comes on, the building is still standing. I get the answering machine. She calls me at work to let me know she's okay. I thank God.

About a month later, I get home from a meeting and notice the light blinking on my answering machine.

"Hi, guys, it's me." My daughter's voice fills the room. "We're under a tornado watch, and I'm going storm chasing. I'm so excited!"

Still I feel no fear. The next morning I hear on the news that an F-5 tornado devastated Oklahoma City and parts of Kansas the night before—a few hours south of where she is. She calls me at work to let me know she's still on the ground. I breathe a prayer of thanks.

Today she leaves Kansas to come home for the summer. She has twenty-two hours of driving ahead of her. She'll be traveling alone—but not alone, really.

You see, from the time we left her standing, 2,200 miles from home, on a curb in Montana a year ago, she has never been alone. For God, in answer to my daily prayers, has given His angels charge over her, to guard her in all her ways—whether she knows it or not.

I know I sure do.

Thank You, Father, for the peace and assurance only You can give. Amen.

ANOTHER MINUTE
Read & meditate on Psalm 34.

What's Left of Christmas?

The grass withers and the flowers fall,
but the word of our God stands forever.
—Isaiah 40:8 NIV

I plopped down on the love seat after the kids left for school and sighed. Another Christmas come and gone. The garlands, holly, and wreaths deck the walls and doors no more. Candles no longer guard against the early winter darkness. The mail brings no cards from faraway friends and relatives, only bills. The house is quieter now, after numerous holiday get-togethers. All that's left of Christmas is one pathetic poinsettia plant in the corner of the living room. Christmas has been packed away for another year. Things are back to normal.

Well, almost. I've got nearly three weeks of daily devotional readings to catch up on, and I'm already five days behind on the "Read the Bible Through in One Year" schedule. I could skip the extra readings, but I don't want to. I'm afraid I'll miss something.

Reading God's Word seems to lay a good, solid foundation for the whole day. Between the lines of these finger-worn pages I find peace, joy, love, faith, and—yes—even patience and self-control. I don't fly off the handle when things start coming at me from every direction, like the day the toaster burned the toast, the commode overflowed, the dog asserted his territorial rights on the carpet, and the vacuum cleaner broke—again.

Reading God's Word, I find that, unlike my Christmas bills, I'll never get a bill for the debt I owe God. His Son already paid it in full. I am assured that I'll never be alone, for God will never leave me. I learn of a darkness much worse than the long winter nights I'm beginning to dislike, but that darkness can be dispelled by the Light of the Son. I read that I'll spend eternity in a place where there is no death, mourning, crying, or pain. And whatever I need, whether it be strength to endure things gone wrong, guidance for a decision, wisdom to handle my teenagers, or a physical need such as food or clothes, my Father in heaven will provide it for me.

I guess Christmas hasn't been packed away, after all, only its outward symbols. Each time I open my Bible, I unwrap another gift.

Thank You, Father, that I can take Christmas with me each day of the New Year every time I read Your Word. Amen.

ANOTHER MINUTE

Read & meditate on Psalm 19:7-11.

Old Timer's Disease

Even though our outward man is perishing, yet the inward man is being renewed day by day.

—2 Corinthians 4:16 NKJV

I seem to be forgetting things more than usual these days. My friend, Sam, calls it "Old Timer's Disease." I don't particularly care to be reminded that I'm inching toward the half-century mark, but the evidence glares me in the face every day. I write myself notes to jar my memory, drink orange juice to jolt my metabolism, and walk a mile a day to combat those extra pounds. Sometimes, though, I still feel I'm fighting a losing battle, especially when I misplace the notes and pig out on cookies at bedtime.

Yet, in spite of all this, I still wouldn't want to be young again. In fact, I kind of like myself the way I am. I know I'm more patient, and I don't lose my temper as quickly nor as much as I did when I was younger. I tend to think things through carefully and not act as impulsively as I once did. And I don't talk as much as I used to because I've learned the value of listening.

Looking back, I can see God's hand on my life and how He used events I thought frustrating or unbearable at the time to mold me into a better person—on the inside, which is more important, anyway. St. Paul referred to our inner person as "treasures in earthen vessels" (2 Corinthians 4:7 NKJV). On the outside, I may feel as though I'm suffering from "Old Timer's Disease," but on the inside, I'm being renewed every day.

Lord, when I start complaining about all my aches and pains, remind me of the treasure You've invested in my soul. Amen.

ANOTHER MINUTE
Read & meditate on 2 Corinthians 4:7—5:1.

Cross or Chorus

Purify my motives, Lord;
replace myself with Thyself.

Ah, can You do this painlessly,
so I don't have to grieve
the death of self?

Replace the cross with a chorus,
so I can sing, not weep;
rejoice, not mourn;
feel wholeness, not brokenness.

Or
perhaps the cross and the chorus
go together.
For
without the cross
there'd be no chorus.

Prayer for the New Year

"My Presence will go with you, and I will give you rest."
—Exodus 33:14 NIV

As I stand on the threshold of a new year, the memories of the old year wrap around me like a cozy patchwork quilt. Dark, light, dull, and bright patches all blend together just as the sorrows, disappointments, joys, and triumphs weave together to form the fabric of my life. And just as a warm sheet of flannel underlies the patches so carefully pieced together, so, Father, You have been there, undergirding every event with Your presence.

When my mother-in-law suffered a heart attack and underwent open-heart surgery, You were there in the friends and family who drove hours on wintry roads to visit. And in the friend who opened his wallet and slipped us a twenty-dollar bill—his last—because he knew we needed a hot meal.

When my daughter was rushed to the hospital after a serious car accident, You were there in both our pastor who dropped what he was doing and hurried to the emergency room, getting there even before the ambulance, and in the friend who followed me to the hospital to make sure I got there safely.

And You were there, Father, when my son flew off a dirt bike and needed eight stitches below his knee, right at the start of all-star practice. Thank You that it wasn't any worse and he got to play baseball—the love of his life—all summer. It kept him out of trouble.

And when the alternator belt on the motor home broke climbing a mountain a hundred miles from home, You were there in the young man who just happened to be hanging out at the gas station where we pulled off. He drove my husband ten miles to the nearest auto parts store and didn't want anything for his trouble.

And when I braked suddenly on a rain-slick road and lost control of the van, You somehow helped me get it back on the road. My children were with me. And on that cold November night when the skies were spitting freezing rain and the roads were a sheet of ice, You got my son and me safely home over thirteen miles of mountain roads, even though my studded tires were still in the garage.

And as I watched my oldest leave the nest, You assured me that You would go with him. Thank You for the fine young man he is becoming, and thank You for the young woman who has agreed to be his wife. She is an answer to this mother's prayer.

Yet even as these patches give comfort and warmth as I face the uncertainties of the new year, I know I must leave them behind and piece together a new quilt. These patches, too, will be dark and light, dull and bright. But underlying them all with be Your presence, and tying them all together will be Your love. Thank You.

ANOTHER MINUTE

Read & meditate on Psalm 139.

Quilting

Discarded dreams,
like clothes that no longer fit,
bagged up,
put away
in the attic of yesterday.

Colors faded,
seams softly strained
from the weight
of a thousand life-cares;
wrinkled, tired, shapeless now,
these dreams that were mine.

But make them over
to warm the cold night.
In patches of color,
blend dark threads with bright.
Old dreams, like old clothes,
reshaped, rearranged,
can be used once again.

"For I know the plans I have for you,"
declares the LORD,
"plans to prosper you and not to harm you.
Plans to give you hope and a future."
Jeremiah 29:11 NIV

Jesus' Cross

Even in the darkest night,
When I just turn and toss,
When all seems hopeless—nothing's right—
I remember Jesus' cross.

That beam of lumber cut to size,
Too heavy to be borne
By One who stepped to Calvary's call
Beaten, mocked, and scorned.

In the shadow of that cross,
How can I complain?
I have not sweat great drops of blood,
I've not endured such pain.

I've had no nails pierce tender flesh,
And no one's spit on me.
No soldier's opened up my back
Nor stabbed my side with glee.

No jeering crowd shouts "Crucify!"
Such loneliness I can't feel.
Yet love for me was the reason why
He bled—and I was healed.

And by His stripes we are healed.
Isaiah 53:5 NKJV

Michele T. Huey is the editor and a feature writer for her local newspaper, *The Punxsutawney Spirit,* where she writes a weekly feature column, "People Who Make a Difference," and a weekly devotional column, "Minute Meditations," which also appears weekly in *The Montgomery Independent* newspaper. In addition, she writes devotionals on assignment for *Pathways to God* and has written Sunday school curriculum for Christian Ed. Publishers. She has been published in national publications such as *Teachers in Focus, Guideposts, Home Life, The Upper Room, Standard,* and *Purpose* and is a contributor to *God's Vitamin C for the Spirit of Women, God's Abundance: 365 Days to Simplify Your Life,* and *Why Fret That God Stuff?* compiled by Kathy Collard Miller and *Chicken Soup for the Christian Family Soul.*

Michele created, wrote, edited and published *That's Write!* a monthly newsletter for the Punxsutawney Area Christian Writers' Fellowship, which she founded and leads. An amateur musician, Michele has composed (music and lyrics) several gospel songs, two of which have been published under the Anjosa label.

In 1997, Michele created "Heartstrings" to self-publish original poetry on bookmarks and plaques, which were sold in local bookstores and consignment shops. She also developed and self-published a teaching unit on the newspaper for junior high or middle school. The unit has been used in schools as part of the Newspaper in Education program and also as home school curriculum.

Michele was the winner of the Jean Berg Memorial Award, given to identify and encourage talented writers, at the 1997 St. Davids Christian Writers Conference. A 1972 graduate of Clarion University of Pennsylvania with a BS in secondary education in the field of comprehensive English, Michele taught English for twelve years, has taught journalism and creative writing classes, and conducted a workshop on writing for the local newspaper at the 1999 St. Davids Christian Writers' Conference.

A wife, mother of three, and grandmother, Michele lives in Smithport with her husband, Dean, and youngest son, David.

Order Additional Copies
for Family and Friends

$8.99 plus $2.00 shipping and handling
(Pennsylvania residents add 6% sales tax)

Send check or money order to:

Michele T. Huey
121 Homestead Lane
Glen Campbell, PA 15742

Inquire about quantity discounts